UNREQUITED LOVE:
A HEART TORN IN TWO

Jeremy Adams

Alpha Publishing, LLC

www.adamswriter.com

Ordering Information:

Quantity sales. Special discounts are available on quantity purchases by corporations, associations, and others. For details, contact the publisher at the address above.

Orders by U.S. trade bookstores and wholesalers. Please contact/visit www.adamswriter.com

Printed in the United States of America

UNREQUITED LOVE-

Love that is not openly reciprocated or understood as such by the beloved. The beloved may not be aware of the admirer's deep and strong romantic affection, or may consciously reject it.

TABLE OF CONTENTS

Preface   1

Introduction   16

The Meaning of Love   25

Heartbreaks, Heartaches   48

Daydreams and Nightmares   72

Reality Check   104

Love Bipolar   119

Forgotten Love   134

What Is Love   142

Unrequited   157

PREFACE

For the sake of this story,

There is no need for my name,

For my story and your story,

Could be one in the same.

I say this for sure,

Without an ounce of hesitation,

That love does not exist,

This is my heart's proclamation.

My friends please listen,

For the notion of love is bizarre,

Flawed in fact,

Just observe from afar.

Or better yet listen to me,

I do know a few facts,

For I loved once before,

Now to love I turn my back.

And don't call me crazy,

For love is far from bliss,

The beginning of the end,

The start of a psychosis.

A psychosis that I endured,

One that I try to ignore,

Yet there is a schism I feel,

A schism that rocked my very core.

After meeting love,

I realized my heart was torn in two,

A split that sadly caused,

This psychosis to accrue.

I still shudder at the thoughts,

The thoughts that feel my mind,

For if love did exist,

Then I'd want it to be mine.

But it is nothing more than a game,

The battle of the sexes,

For in the end we are all alone,

We all end up as exes.

So why waste time,

Why even bother with dreams,

Wishing for love and happiness,

But love is far from what it seems.

And take it from me,

I fell in love with love,

I feign for that feeling,

I was born to love.

But as time progressed,

I began to see a fatal flaw,

That the truth in love,

Will leave you in awe.

As a matter of fact,

The truth in love is really a lie,

A convoluted way of thinking

One that many should deny.

For as I said before,

There is no need to share my name,

For my story and your story,

Could be one in the same.

This is a story about love,

But far from a love story ,

Beware my friends,

For this could get a bit gory.

Pray tell me this,

If love is completely true,

Then why am I sitting here?

With a heart torn in two.

But I know with certainty,

That I'm not alone,

Many of us have realized,

That our hearts would never have a home,

This story is yours, and mine,

A story of unrequited sin,

Where you give your all,

Only to have your world cave in.

For that is the idea of love,

Where you give someone your all,

Your body soul and mind,

A key with the permission to fall.

Sadly you have no control,

In who reciprocates this feeling,

For if this were possible,

Then love would be more appealing.

But ever since love lost its appeal,

It began to cease to exist,

And with these words I speak truth,

To you and I love will not be missed.

For I am more than ready,

To enjoy my life,

And this is so much easier,

Without an emotion that causes strife.

Some may think I hate love,

They must have a wild imagination,

For they believe in a lie,

But I find truth in liberation.

No longer am I captive,

To the hopes they may have,

For hopeless romantics,

Dream of a love that will never last.

And what is a hopeless romantic,

Please allow me to explain,

It is someone who believes,

True love is their aim.

Before I continue any further,

We must start from the beginning,

Then, maybe then, you'll understand,

Why true love has an ending.

Tread softly my friends,

And please have an open mind,

For you'll see the real truth,

In all due time.

I hope this to be,

A story with a call to action,

That each and every reader,

Denounces this perverse passion.

This perversion that causes,

A chemical reaction in the brain,

That makes you think,

Without him, or her life would not be the same.

My reason in writing this book,

Is to tell the story of the unknown,

A story of pain and despair,

Where love's sins are left un-atoned.

A story where you wish,

With all of your power and might,

That you never heard of love,

For it is soon followed by plight.

I write this book in hopes,

That you will learn from my mistake,

That you change your mind

Before it's all too late.

I have seen the tears,

Love is not what you think,

And no matter what you've been told,

Two souls can never be in sync.

My friends I am quite sadly,

Incapable of ever loving again,

I wish I knew why,

I wish I could make amends.

For I tried love once,

You may find this hard to believe,

Some of you may even think,

That true love was not achieved.

For if it was,

I wouldn't be telling this tale,

But o my friends it was,

That's why life is a living hell.

And that's why forever,

I will denounce the world's biggest lie,

I wish I were wrong,

But no longer will I try.

If I could put into words,

The pain that I feel,

I'd lose my life,

For these words would kill.

And to some of us, the unlucky ones,

Happiness was never an option,

But we had no clue,

So we proceeded without caution.

So young and innocent,

Thinking that dreams come true,

So we dreamt the most dreamt dream of all,

Falling in love with that special You.

Some think they find true love,

But they find another willing to settle,

Convincing themselves they're in love,

Displaying a cowardly mettle.

For they would rather lie to themselves,

And accept what is then what could be,

With only one life to live,

They choose to never be free.

Love is a death sentence,

A life without parole,

Give someone your all forever,

Relinquish all control.

My sentiment on love,

Is one you rarely hear,

For what is the point in living,

If love is what you fear.

And I have asked myself this question,

Is life really worthwhile?

Maybe we lie to ourselves,

But I am here to put love on trial.

Excuse me for my rant,

But you all needed to know my reason,

My reason for writing this book,

For love committed high treason.

It has betrayed you and I,

Leaving us dazed and confused,

It is time to tell this story,

Of love's wicked ruse.

Love is wicked,

A statement I realized too late,

But as the story develops,

You will begin to see my fate.

I caution you my friends,

This story may bring tears,

It is a story that is true,

Filled with doubt, hate, and fear.

But as most stories go,

The result was never meant to be,

In the beginning you'll find,

I wanted to love desperately.

This is the type of story,

That will touch your soul,

Cause you to question truth,

May even take its toll.

First let me set the premise,

While young I fell in love with love,

Consumed I was by the thought of it,

A notion I hoped to never be free of.

Yes, I too at one time

Wanted to be love's captive,

It was my purpose in life,

A deep desire that was massive.

I dreamt of it forever,

But soon encountered it in reality,

What I had dreamt for so long,

Soon resulted in fatality.

Death to my dreams,

Death to it all,

Death to my happiness,

Death to Love's thrall.

So sit back and listen,

Try not to fight the truth,

For if you think I am lying,

My story will show proof.

And so here I am,

It is time for the story to begin,

Unrequited Love: A Heart Torn in Two,

Where love met its end.

INTRODUCTION

A heart torn in two beware love's woes,

For pain from love caused dismember,

The mistake I made when I gave love my rose,

Is one that I would always remember.

A heart torn in two led to dissent in my soul,

For I wanted to know love forever,

Yet love tore apart my dream and my goal,

Now my dreams must reside with never.

A heart torn in two from honest lies,

Still love visits me in various forms,

Sadly, "love" is now what I despise,

Lust, the new love-sadly the new norm.

A heart torn in two should I love again?

For a love so true is now gone with the wind

Residue from the past makes it hard to mend,

And this is how my heart met its end.

For I often feared that my past would haunt me,

Yet haunting is more of an understatement,

Consumption is the correct word you see,

The past wants to be my present's replacement.

I can't blame the past for this,

For life was simple back then,

A life so simple it's easy to miss,

Reminisce I do oft with a grin.

The kid inside wants to be free,

Yet what does that even mean,

I look in the mirror and I see,

The residue left from a dream.

A dream that started in a young child,

One that lit up his world,

Now it seems life has gotten too wild,

This dream is really about a girl.

A girl any girl in fact,

Whom I could give my heart to,

For love has changed the way I act,

And changed my world's view.

I only had one heart to give,

And I gave it all to love,

Afraid I am I no longer live,

Something I am not particularly proud of.

For I had heard about,

The allure of love's doings,

And even though I used to doubt,

I still proceeded to wooing.

My first encounter with love,

Was quite unique and rare,

For this encounter I'm speaking of,

I never knew it would be too much to bare.

But now I wonder around aimlessly,

I have for these past few years of my life,

Looking for a girl shamelessly,

To give my heart a new life.

But my heart cannot be revived,

By just a random lady,

I fear I can no longer survive,

In a world where love is now so shady.

For I was born with one dream,

To love another forever,

Sadly it appears to seem,

That my heart can only stay severed.

No longer do I know what to do,

My dream has been taken away,

The girls in this world are few,

Causing my heart dismay.

Few-for not many can replace her,

Far-the ones that can I pay no mind,

True-at times I do begin to infer,

Why these girls do not compare to mine.

For I courted love for many years,

Of course back in my younger days,

Looked past the hurt and fears,

For she had left me in a daze.

Soon however it ended,

No longer was she there to be,

And the girl named love I befriended,

Was no longer meant for me.

So what was once mine,

Soon became another's,

I would like to say I am fine,

But at times, I still want to love her.

You see what once was is no more,

And it is still hard to accept this fact,

That what is gone I still yearn for,

Deep down I yearn to have my heart back.

But how can my heart be retrieved,

What more will love take,

She has left me alone to grieve,

Treachery soon led to my heartbreak.

At times in my life I began to wonder why,

Why am I such a feign,

For love to me has said goodbye,

Yet one side forever screams.

So to get my heart back what shall I do,

To stubborn I am to love another,

Sadly my heart has been torn in two,

Yet I gave both sides to my ex lover.

Chasing I am a love I once knew,

However love does not give back,

 I thought what we had was once so true,

The faith I had in love I now lack.

The dilemma is-I want love again,

But solving the problem is hard,

Being alone will never end,

Too hurt I am to let down my guard.

What happens when love cannot be returned?

And you have given your heart away,

Earth becomes a place where you burn,

A place where I am destined to stay.

I cannot leave this hell on earth,

Believe me my friends I have tried,

Ironically enough I knew her worth,

But in the end, she never complied.

What happens after heartbreak?

Well you will soon find out,

Careful – it may cause heartache

My story turns hope into doubt.

I fell for unparalleled beauty,

Years ago as a young man,

Took it as my own duty,

To love beyond a certain span.

So proceed with caution as you read this tale,

Yearn I do for just one simple wish,

Wish I do that I never fell,

For love put my heart at risk.

Make no mistake for years we were one,

And for years my life was complete,

But one day love decided to run,

I stood there in awe and defeat.

THE MEANING OF LOVE

As most people in this world,

I too searched for meaning,

For me, it was a girl,

For you it could be healing.

For this world has a lot of pain,

And we all find ways to cope,

At times we can be driven insane,

But at the end of the day we still have hope.

I have often wondered,

What exactly is the meaning of love?

At nights I even pondered,

What it is we dream of.

For I know that most if not all,

Do want to know this feeling,

For if you do recall,

Love is quite appealing.

But why must we search for meaning in another,

I have tried so hard to understand,

I look and see couples all over each other,

Thinking that P.D.A should be banned.

But I do have a notion,

One that may give reason,

For maybe the meaning of this strange emotion,

Is to give color to our seasons.

For we go throughout this life,

Dull and emotionless to say the least,

Filled with so much strife,

For who can give us peace.

However, soon you find someone,

Who can help you take away the pain,

True love has soon begun,

Now you are one in the same.

What is the meaning of love?

Words could never truly explain,

But I could try my best to speak of,

Why love should forever reign.

To me the sound of love's name,

Is one that is the sweetest melody?

It is one that quickly sets my heart aflame,

Just hearing love's name is therapy.

With love, dreams can never compare,

For love far exceeds one's idealizations,

On sight when you see love you slowly lose air,

This is a sign, for that's your heart's declaration.

To me, love will never grow old,

It is in fact something that will last forever,

And when you have it what a sight to behold,

Once two strangers now united together.

To me, love shows you your truest form,

By loving another you are soon revealed,

The masks to society that you have worn,

Are forever now concealed.

To me, love says its okay to be you,

For deep down love really wants you to see,

That no matter what happens it will always be true,

To the bond of You and Me.

The meaning of love is quite profound,

One that you will never completely know,

At times love may even leave some dumbfound,

But there is always room to grow.

This is what I think love means,

And we all have our different notions,

Joy and happiness, we all dream,

So the thought of love keeps our heart open.

And to me that is a brief version,

Of what I think love really means,

So I embarked on a little excursion,

To find the love of my dreams.

Sadly however, the beginning of my amour,

Did lead to my untimely demise,

For the end of my love happened before,

I even knew of love's lies.

To help you understand the end,

You must first know the correlation,

The omega of my love did begin,

With my heart's proclamation.

Proclaiming that she was the one,

As soon as our paths collided,

My first thought was to simply run,

But her beauty left me blinded.

For a while I was too shy to approach,

Because of the fear of rejection,

Afraid I would be reproached,

But my friend had a suggestion.

He asked me what did I have to lose,

Honestly I did not know,

Maybe my legs might refuse,

But my heart could not let her go.

A beauty too daunting for me to chase,

I decided to adore from afar,

Love enveloped in my heart's sacred place,

I concluded that she was my star.

My sun that is for she lit up my world,

Warmed up my soul and brighten my days,

I had no choice but to make her my girl,

Or forever my heart would be hazed.

Let me explain to you all,

For this beauty was unique,

One with an alluring call,

Consumed with a little mystique.

My whole life I had seen,

This thing called beauty,

Yet in my wildest dreams,

I never thought it would consume me.

For I thought I knew beauty then I saw her,

And beauty as a human could not outdo,

What she had, left beauty to infer,

When it came to beauty, beauty had no clue.

I thought I knew beauty then I saw her,

She replaced beauty and took her throne,

The old beauty began to defer,

To the girl I had hoped to make my own.

I thought I knew beauty then I saw her,

And I knew I had to make her mine,

For she outdid beauty and I prefer,

To have the girl that made beauty resign.

Imagine that for me,

This girl the beauty queen,

Sounds like a delightful story,

Boy gets girl of his dreams.

Unfortunately I could not resist,

And sadly I could not deny,

For I now had a reason to exist,

And to give love a try.

So I approached this girl,

Or you can call her beauty,

With the truism to give her the world,

And to love her as my life's duty.

Maybe just maybe ,

I could give her a rose for her heart,

Announce to the world, "there's my baby,"

For once we knew love we'd never part.

For the day I saw her I could not believe,

The beauty she had managed to achieve,

Caused me to think my eyes were deceived,

Because of her –in me-love was conceived,

Too shy I was to be in her presence,

A queen she was-I was just a peasant,

Cautiously I approached her with reverence,

With a rose to give as a present.

The rose I gave her was a symbol of my heart,

It was to become our way of life,

May we unite together and never grow apart,

May our love bring harmony and never strife,

The rose I gave her contained many thorns,

But it was also a symbol of my affection

Make it through each thorn -true love is born,

May we share something special -an unworldly connection,

The rose I gave her may it never fade away,

For love for me means forever,

I planted the rose in her heart where I wanted it to stay,

For we would share infinity together.

She took the rose with preconceived notions,

Premature apologies for her guarded wall,

Warning me that her heart had been broken,

When it came to love she never wanted to fall.

A fall in love-she was a bit skeptic,

But in me she would find a love she deserved,

"I don't know," she said "my heart's decrepit,"

But to love another would be absurd.

Reciprocate she would the love I gave,

For she said I was different from other guys she met,

She turned to her friends and began to rave,

For she knew with me she would not fret.

As I walked away I gave her a kiss,

Not on the lips you see for I take things slow,

On her cheek, that is, purposely I missed,

Move too fast and love will not grow.

Move too fast and lust will accrue,

But there is a secret you need to know,

Patience breeds love-love breeds from two,

And I gave my love to her some time ago.

You see, some people believe in love at first sight,

But I knew her before she knew me,

At times I would see her at night,

That is, in my dreams you see.

It's hard to explain what I felt,

When I finally saw her for the first time,

Almost as if my heart already dwelt,

In a girl who had yet to be mine.

So how could I use the word love?

On a girl that I hardly even know

Sent to me she was from above,

We just needed some time to grow.

And here is where my dreams came true,

For I had never wanted anything more,

True love found so early who knew,

That I would love her so deeply to her core.

Finally I had been given,

A chance to experience love,

A love where I was completely smitten,

For it was everything I had dreamed of.

It was the start of a love never known to man,

One that was growing with more emotion,

A love so coveted but part of my plan,

Even with the non- stop commotion.

For the world wanted us to fail,

They tried to feed us lies,

And even with the world's creative tales,

Love, for me, I'd never despise.

It was hard for me to even believe,

That before I met her I was so lost,

A life so cruel-in her-I found reprieve,

No longer wondering this world with extreme exhaust.

But unconditional love had grown in me,

The bond we had could never be broken,

Our love on display for the world to see,

Our relationship soon became love's token.

Time went by but our love remained,

For we saw a future- a tomorrow,

Never did we know love in vain,

So we loved past the hurt and sorrow,

I'd be remised to say we never fought,

Yet with each fight our love grew,

Together still look what love has brought,

A bond so strong-a love so true,

Two souls collided with one emotion,

Me plus her- together we make one,

United we were with devout devotion,

Our heart's united true love begun.

Devoted I was to showing her,

That fairy tales do exist,

And then I began to infer,

True love began to desist.

My pursuit to obtain her heart,

No –I wanted more-her soul,

I wanted a love that could never part,

I wanted only her to make me whole.

Coveted she was for her beauty alone,

Her beauty alone was divine,

Safe she was in my heart-her home,

To reside elsewhere would be a crime.

She had her preconceived notions,

But I told her she could confide in me,

Even though relationships today seem broken,

For us this would never be.

In my arms I promised her protection,

And may we never ever part,

She said she's lost I'd give her direction,

Just the follow the road to my heart.

But if she happened to put up a wall,

I would gladly break it down,

Boast to the world that she is my all,

And I'd give to her this crown.

This crown would represent her as my queen,

And she could never give it away,

I could show her a love that's never been seen,

My love for her would never decay.

We would sit and talk about aspirations,

I remember one night so vividly,

Maybe it was best to set a foundation,

So I told love what she meant to me.

I told love that she was my dream,

And that I would sacrifice anything for her,

I held her heart with such high esteem,

Ecstatic for what we were.

She blushed as I told her my dream,

I waited to see what she had to say,

She thought I had developed a nice scheme,

A scheme to steal her heart away.

Her dream was to marry,

A man that was like no other,

She was beginning to grow wary,

Until she found me, her eternal lover.

Her dream was to know amour,

In ways never thought possible,

Maybe the idea of her dream and more,

Should not have been plausible.

That was until the day she met me,

The nightmares she soon did bid adieu,

Her dreams soon became a reality,

Love soon began to accrue.

"What is my dream?" she said "my dream is you,

Actually my dream is us,

Our love in fact is o so true,

To you, I give my heart with trust."

I accepted her heart with pleasure,

In awe I was of this possession,

I loved her with such leisure,

That day she became my obsession.

Obsessed I was in a healthy way,

Every man should obsess to some degree,

It lets her know the price you will pay,

To be with a girl as beautiful as she.

That day I will forever remember,

For our love did truly ascend,

Thought our souls would never dismember,

Thought our love would know no end.

Whenever I would see her, my heart would race,

I could not even believe she was mine,

A love so daunting it was worth the chase,

Forever this love will be on my mind.

Every part of my day revolved around her,

I tried to keep it to myself but I had a confession,

Thought love was a lie but no longer I concur,

She had stolen my heart and became my obsession.

Sadly, once I knew this,

I had lost complete control,

For my obsession was something I would soon miss,

My obsession soon caused my world to fold.

I once heard that whoever cares the least,

Has the most power of the two,

What was once love began to cease,

For she held the power through and through.

I made the mistake,

For love I delve into,

And maybe my confession was far too late,

For me to ever undo.

You see my friends the meaning,

The meaning of love I did once obtain,

Caused me to see that I was hopelessly dreaming,

For a notion that no longer remained.

I thought love meant,

You would always rise above the fray,

The notion of love had always left me content,

Soon I would find that love had gone away.

In hindsight I do realize,

That I cared too much,

This led to my demise,

For my heart soon needed a crutch.

Now the meaning of love to me,

Is quite contrary to what was first said,

In the beginning I thought this wouldn't be,

But in the end I'd agree love is dead.

Herein lies a transition,

How I went from love's advocate to foe,

And please spare me the opposition,

My friends you still have much to know.

To me, love was the only thing,

I could completely believe in,

Hope was all I had to bring,

And I thought forever knew no end.

To me, love was the sum,

Of everything that was right in this world,

For all the negativity felt was soon numb,

When I laid eyes on this girl.

That was the meaning of love to me,

But as humans we all make mistakes,

The one I made soon allowed me to see,

That my thoughts for love were far too great.

But I had heard stories ever since I was born

Of the world's greatest prize,

Love, they said, can truly transform,

Yet they never warned me of love's disguise.

My friends before I met love,

The meaning of it I romanticized,

For what I once used to speak so highly of,

Had yet to be analyzed.

My meaning of love did change,

After love and I's first meeting,

I soon became deranged,

Life was slowly depleting.

You see I never knew love could end,

But I arrived to this conclusion too late,

Just when my love really did begin,

I was introduced to heartbreak.

Love I soon found,

Was such a twisted notion,

For what I thought was forever bound,

Soon caused extreme commotion.

A love I once owned,

I soon no longer professed,

Slowly love became unknown,

To the heart I once possessed.

HEARTBREAKS, HEARTACHES

I am sure most if not all,

Can undoubtedly relate,

You became a victim to the fall,

And the damage love creates.

And this is how love can only end,

With heartbreaks, treachery, and lies,

Foolishly I thought I could make amends,

With a notion I now despise.

I could see for a while,

That our relationship would soon be over,

Her demeanor towards me was slightly vile,

But I still held my composure.

I cannot lie I was a hopeless romantic,

So I always thought I could make her see,

That with what we had there was no need to panic,

For what we had would always be.

Sadly however she continued to push me away,

But never had the courage to say goodbye,

The situation I was in, left me in complete dismay,

But for love I would continue to try.

But there was only so much I could ignore,

The pain was becoming too much to bare,

I continued to love her but what for,

The love she once had for me was no longer there.

I began to laugh at the four-letter word she would say to me,

Loving for me had become a pain,

She said it all the time but I could not see,

Forgive me as I continue to complain.

Love is easy yet she made it complex,

What must be done, for my love to be returned?

Unrequited love has left me a bit perplexed,

And it has left me a bit concerned.

Love with her was hell and I continued to burn,

Maybe it is best if we continued to part,

Still I would wait for her heart in return,

But the waiting was breaking my heart,

But I could not let her go,

And I didn't know how fix us or where to begin,

For without her, life I would never know,

But my unrequited love would soon be coming to an end.

And with that declaration,

A fight was soon ensuing,

My heart wanted reparations,

Maybe the fight was my doing.

I couldn't hold it in,

And she was getting a bit perturbed,

Soon her quietness did end,

And her temper left me quite disturbed.

For I would yell, she would scream- o what a fight,

One that was quite disturbing to see,

I knew where I would be that night,

Finally away from her sadly,

I would fight and argue because I wanted more,

Maybe this argument would soon subside,

At least I knew what I was fighting for,

For with her is where I wanted to reside.

I hoped the fight would cause our love to grow,

I hoped she would find a way to love me better,

I hoped we were too strong for love's foes,

Hoped our bond would forever be tethered.

I yelled she screamed, it was another fight,

But I hoped we could love during stormy weather,

And soon our love would reach new heights,

Soon our love would only get better.

But I was wrong for our love did not,

Our fights continued to grow,

The fighting is what soon begot,

Our bond to take a huge blow.

What are the stages of heartbreak?

Well I'm glad someone finally asked,

It seems as if I was too late,

To save my girl from her past.

Little did I know about her past,

Unfortunately I soon found out,

Because of this it was hard to last,

For when it came to love she was in doubt.

Inevitably she would soon leave,

I knew this some time ago,

In my soul I found it hard to believe,

But deep down I knew she would let go.

When she declared her love for me,

I assume she was caught by surprise,

And for her it became hard to see,

For her past continued to reprise.

But not by circumstance,

See perception is it all,

And neither by happenstance,

Did she end up building a wall.

Never had she seen a love so true,

And I talk about the love in us,

Confused she wondered what to do,

She never knew a man she could trust.

A broken home caused her to believe,

That when it comes to love to despise,

For the "love" she saw did deceive,

Her heart and caused her to see true lies.

I could sense she was beginning to fear,

And I could feel us falling apart,

I needed her to be completely sincere,

I needed to know where her heartbreak starts.

She replied and asked, "What is true?"

For love she believed was not,

Her parents once loved but now bid adieu,

She once knew love now she forgot.

"No don't forget love," I replied,

"Take a look at you and me,"

Slowly she hung her head and cried,

"I am afraid of love now you see."

"Inevitably love will end," she said,

"Love met its end in my parent's eyes,

My mama's heart was torn to shred,

Thanks to love's clever lies.

And hold on there is even more,

For why this troubles my soul,

My father's heart did once adore,

My mother who made him whole.

Adore, like you claim to adore me,

But you see how their love ends,

In love I was with the thought of we,

Now it is best that we just be friends."

No way I could be just friends with her,

The thought of it attacked my heart,

Being alone I did not prefer,

I begged her to not part.

Unfortunately the damage was done,

I was punished for her parent's sins,

The heartbreak had now begun,

My world had met its end.

Usually I am not the one to plead,

But I could not say goodbye,

So I swallowed my pride and began to proceed,

To explain to her the reason why.

The reason why she should believe,

That with love there is no need to fret,

She already had my heart, there's no way I could retrieve,

Giving her my heart I soon did regret.

For if I knew love would lie,

There would have never been a beginning,

Now I sit here trying to avoid love's goodbye,

For it seems this is an inevitable ending.

But maybe I could convince her,

And love would see my sincerity,

For this love had become my anchor,

So I explained my sentiment with clarity.

Whatever she wanted I would give to her,

When times got rough our love would stand

 She wanted goodbye but I prayed she defer,

For I'd give her my heart just to hold her hand

Never leave me no matter how rough things might be,

For I will never be able to say goodbye,

This pain will soon subside just stay with me,

But if she had to leave my heart would forever cry.

Sadly it seems a split is coming,

And I have tried my best to avoid this,

I kept chasing cause she kept running,

Our love would soon be in an abyss.

This love the one I gave my all,

Has caused a split I never imagined,

I knew it was best for me to avoid the fall,

But a beauty such as hers was a distraction.

I hoped my broken heart would one day mend,

For I now see that there is nothing I could do,

My heart torn in two could not be how we end,

Without love I question what is true.

But she did not listen to my plea,

To hurt she was by what she had seen,

And all the love I had with she,

Was soon gone as was my dream.

A breakup one not foreseen,

But what was next for me,

All my life I had dreamt this dream,

Where love and I would be.

So what is there for me to do?

Run around to find a love that replenishes,

For I thought I had love but it never made its cue,

To me this thing called "love" diminishes.

It diminishes everything that life is about,

And my first encounter was disheartening,

For what I thought about love I now doubt,

The scary truth is now alarming.

Or maybe I did not meet love,

Upon my first encounter with this girl,

For it is something we should not speak of,

For maybe love is not of this world.

But the heartbreak I am feeling,

Is far from undeniable,

Love is no longer appealing,

And my life, no longer viable.

Heartbreak, I never thought we'd meet,

So now the pain is unbelievable,

Heartbreak on its way to greet,

A boy who thought this pain was inconceivable.

Heartbreak, upon our first meeting,

I soon realized the scary truth,

The forces inside of me competing,

For a life far better than what I had in youth.

Apparently, there are five stages of heartbreak,

Disheartenment is number one,

For my future now seemed opaque,

My relationship was now done.

But maybe I could see her again,

Maybe our love would be reborn

For true love could have no end,

But If I am wrong, love I will scorn.

So maybe I should be optimistic,

Maybe I will see her later,

Or maybe this is unrealistic,

Maybe I should just hate her.

But If I ever lost her, my heart would eternally be resting,

Laying dormant until the next time love came around,

To be in her presence was a blessing,

That day we said goodbye but our hearts were still bound.

My heart was slowly decaying as we sat there together,

Even after all the pain that she put me through,

My pulse slowly fading-there goes my forever,

I wonder what it is I should do.

Even though I can see the writings on the wall,

I still wonder why I have yet to cry,

Maybe its because I can still hear her heart call,

Shed a tear? No –optimism is why.

Optimism huh, denial is two,

This stage made me think she'd come back soon,

I once had plenty now I have few,

Optimism led me to my doom.

For years I thought she would come back,

For years I was terribly wrong,

My lust for life began to lack,

The more years that I spent alone.

But back then I was young and naïve,

I stayed on that stage for a while,

Hoping that I would in fact retrieve,

The love that had stolen my smile.

Withdrawal is stage three of this mess,

And it was the hardest one for me,

During this stage I could only guess,

If I'd ever go back to being free.

Free from this love that captured my heart,

A captive I was in my own world,

I cursed cupid for not playing his part,

For his arrow was needed for this girl.

But maybe cupid had known,

Known this for a very long time,

That love in this world was gone,

So sadly he could not make her mine.

However, if you looked in my eyes you would see pain,

For no way I could make it in this cold dreary night,

It's sad to see how love had become a game,

For I tried to turn something wrong into right.

The notion of love I continued to think about,

Even though love had just gone away,

Sadly there was an internal bout,

Left speechless with nothing to say.

Yet here I was strung out on her,

What I would do to hold her one more time,

With all the confusion I did concur,

I'd go through hell and back to make her forever mine.

The worst part of heartbreak,

Would have to be the depression,

For many hours at night I laid awake,

Because of this oppression.

This stage caused me to think,

That loving her was really a lie,

And what I felt made my heart shrink,

To the point where it actually died.

Till this day I tell you,

I thought my love would never know an end,

But then my plan fell through,

My heart no longer I could mend.

Depression leads to a weary life,

Where darkness consumes you every day,

And you become good friends with strife,

Till emotionally you pass away.

Occupied I was with death,

Depression I never let go,

Maybe the next stage would give me breath,

But sadly the answer was no.

Acceptance is the last stage,

But no need to talk about that,

Never was I able to turn the page,

For in retrospect, I always looked back.

And to her, the one I would eternally love,

I still remembered the day I looked into her eyes,

So thankful that she was sent from above,

Made me want to grab her heart and forever make it mines.

Love is not easy it requires a price,

But maybe that price was too costly for her,

Anything worth having requires sacrifice,

A heart torn in two soon did occur.

And never again would there be another us,

Never again would I feel what I felt with she,

Never again would I be able to trust,

Never again would the existence of my heart be.

Never again would there be a girl so beautiful in life,

Never again would I work so hard to break down walls,

Never again would a girl cause me so much strife,

Never again would I give a girl my all,

And never again would love be there,

Never again would I wait for love's cue,

Never again would I have a heart to share,

Never again-I wish what I just said was true.

I know I am lying,

Trying to avoid this pain,

And maybe I am vying,

For a love that will never know my name.

I want to know what love is; love does not want to know me,

Is there something wrong am I asking for too much?

For I want to know what love is but love cannot see,

For me it seems love my heart will never touch.

Now it's hanging on a string waiting to be mended,

The death of my love is what will forever be mourned,

One more heartbreak and a funeral will be attended,

For I cannot continue to love with a heart completely torn.

But I have finally made a decision,

Loving for me was something I must say goodbye to,

And for once I had no choice but to listen,

For my heart only wanted love- but love wasn't true.

Love, to me, would forever hold a place in my heart,

But maybe for her this feeling is not the same,

I pray that we unite together once more and never part,

If this is not true then I must forever live in pain.

Love, had forgotten our past,

Undoubtedly betrayed I was by she,

Sadly there is no way we could last,

Maybe love was not best for me.

How funny how I was there for her,

But love could never be there for me,

Now this dissent continues to occur,

Yet for some reason I still cannot flee.

She must have forgotten that she was my life,

And how no one else could compare to me,

In this crazy world we showed each other what's right,

No one could ever love her so genuinely.

I knew what it took to love someone special as she,

I was there to comfort her when she would weep,

Maybe her and I were never meant to be,

To achieve love for us would be an impossible feat.

Would she ever find another to help her face her fears?

Would there be another who could love so true,

Is there another who would wipe her tears?

When she wanted to know life anew.

Where is the one that would pick her up when she fell,

It appears to me that this love is through,

And all because she put me through hell,

I had no choice but to bid love adieu.

Even with all of the anger inside,

I still could not let love be,

Whenever love needed someone in whom to confide,

I still let love use me.

But it was time to go our separate ways,

O, I never thought I would say this,

And even though a beauty like love's left me in a daze,

The allure of her I must now resist.

But still I heard her voice today how unexpected,

Why do I say I do not care when I know that is a lie?

How long would our love go on neglected?

Why start falling again when I know I must say goodbye?

Should I thank God for a blessing that has gone too soon?

Why think about her with each breath that I take?

If our love was a flower then why has it not bloomed?

Why continue to love when it seems easier to hate?

Why do I still imagine us together?

Why do I still love her when she caused me pain?

Why do I still see us sharing forever?

Why asks why- love has driven me insane?

Yes love or lack thereof,

Had certainly driven me insane,

The heartbreak I tried not to speak of,

Is certainly the one to blame.

I was consumed by heartbreaks and heartaches,

There was no way life could get worst,

I thought I could find a way to save me for my own sake,

But daydreams and nightmares soon disperse.

DAYDREAMS AND NIGHTMARES

The world around me,

Quickly became surreal,

I was questioning reality,

I knew not what was real.

Day in and day out,

I was having an out of body experience,

Faced with an internal bout,

That caused me to be delirious.

In my mind I was with her,

In reality I knew that wasn't true,

But what was soon to occur,

I had to bid adieu,

My relationship was finally over,

But my thoughts never aligned with reality,

I had to find a way to get closure,

Or forever change my mentality.

Sadly I had no idea how to refrain,

From the way I still thought about love,

Even with all the lies and games,

This notion I couldn't help but speak of.

For I knew what I had was true,

And I could not accept the lies,

Nothing in this world could ever do,

What love's beauty did to my eyes.

There were beautiful girls around the world,

But none as beautiful as she,

Love you could call her soon became my girl,

A love that was made for me.

A beauty that was perfect -nonetheless,

The first night I met love I will always remember,

To be in her presence, I was blessed,

Just hearing her voice made my heart tremor,

Our love really did start as a fairy tale,

But now it is time where we must let go,

In her my heart will forever dwell,

Will there be another us? Only Heaven knows.

I can say this cause I feel it in the depths of my soul,

There is a vacant spot I pray she will one day fill,

For without her in my life, my heart will forever have a hole,

And if not her then nobody else will,

I guess it is time to quit

For maybe this is over maybe this is the end,

And this is still hard for me to admit

But if this be true, love is a word I'll never use again.

But I know love,

And deep down she has to still think of me,

For I know this is something she doesn't speak of,

But please take a look and see.

I knew love dreamed of fairy tales,

Well I could be her prince charming,

Must she continue to hide behind her veil?

I wanted her heart without alarming.

She dreamed of this endless love,

Well quite sadly don't we all,

She dreamed of a future in hopes of,

Finally giving into the fall.

I knew she wanted to be together,

But to have a future she could not look in the past,

She said she always dreamt of forever,

Well, here was her slipper made of glass.

She dreamt of a family, I wanted kids too,

And I knew how much she dreamt of security,

I wish she knew I could make her life anew,

But her dreams soon faded into obscurity.

For she once dreamt of life but it had past her by,

But still I'd like to show her how it should be,

She dreamt of perfection, well I'm her dream guy,

Just sitting here waiting for her to see.

I'm sure that she had heard this plenty of times,

See I had something that I wanted to say,

But allow me to get this off my mind,

I wanted to do it in a special way.

How do you tell beauty she is beautiful- I'm sure she knows,

Yet in this case I say that this beauty is rare,

Telling her again would be kind of redundant you know,

Laying eyes on her resulted in me losing air.

So in a way I found a beauty that steals,

My eyes met her and they begin to fall,

First my breath and then my will,

My will to maintain these sturdy walls,

So to the beauty thief, I call her, thanks for life,

For this girl cannot exist in the real world

In my dreams I hope to see her, every night,

In my dreams I see her-I call her my dream girl.

Dreams and nightmares became the norm,

And sadly these two things I could not control,

In my dreams love would take a deceptive form,

And my God what a sight she was to behold.

But I continued to drift,

From what was wrong and right,

Causing an even bigger rift,

In what soon became my chaotic life.

Depression consumed me,

In a way I never thought possible,

Causing me to question my mortality,

The thought, I know, does not seem plausible.

For If I died tonight let this be known,

And hopefully the world will see,

I left this earth without a home,

That the love I once had was never meant to be.

If I died tonight would love feel this pain,

And if she did then please tell her to shed no tears,

For quite honestly, I have not been the same,

Since love left me here.

Time went by-the thought of her consumed me,

Causing me to think our bond was real,

Nightmares and daydreams soon came to be,

So vivid I thought that they were real.

The daydreams gave me hope and more,

Thinking we would soon reunite,

Nightmares had a different plan in store,

Causing despair to dwell in my life.

I soon became divided,

On whether to love or hate,

Dreams and nightmares provided,

For me-a reality escape.

In dreams I was consumed with life,

In nightmares overwhelmed by death,

In dreams I knew what was right,

In nightmares I had nothing left.

Haunted I was in the back of my mind,

With what I call echoes of silence,

Yearning for what was really mine,

Dying from heartbreak's violence.

Do you hear my heart calling for you?

I try to hide it but that I cannot do,

I have every reason not to love but yet I still do,

And this explains why my heart will forever be torn in two.

Echoes of silence-deadly they are,

Luckily I did survive,

How I did was quite bizarre,

Dreams and nightmares kept me alive.

The first nightmare I woke up with chills,

Afraid life could no longer improve,

I viewed my funeral against my will,

My sanity had been removed.

At many times I wondered why,

Why could I not shake this emotion?

For love had yet to even try,

To ever seduce me with her potion.

I wanted to be seduced by love,

Don't we all in some sort of way,

But maybe for me different plans from above,

Caused me to lead my heart astray.

For this disease that was forming,

Was one that was out of my control,

No antidote so I was conforming,

To a man that had truly lost his soul.

And without my soul I could feel it coming,

And sadly I had no clue what to do,

And deep down inside I could feel it spawning,

For a death was coming a death caused by You.

Death is approaching soon it will be near,

But I'm not fleeing for I know not what to do,

And excuse my ignorance but death I do not fear,

For I lost my life when my heart fell for love's coup.

And this was just the beginning,

Really a prelude to a nightmare,

For in this nightmare I saw my ending,

A funeral that was far too much for me to bare.

The Funeral

Here lies a man, who once had everything to live for,

This young man once found life very fulfilling,

But little did he know what life had in store,

For life would give him a premature killing.

This young man never lived too long,

He died unofficially at an early age,

In the flesh here-but everything else gone,

Held on to parts of his life unable to turn the page.

So why are we here to bury him if he died years ago,

The answer I wish was one that I could give,

And truth be told I do not really know,

So if anyone knows please tell us why he no longer lives.

In walked his friend well more like his brother,

Well my friends this day brings sadness to my heart,

Together we shared a bond stronger than any other,

But let me tell you why his death is in two parts.

Yes right there in the basket lays the body of my friend,

My brother wanted a lot in life but only one thing he needed,

During life, he suffered from a death within,

For without this certain thing, his life was depleted.

This need extended beyond his soul,

Love is what I'm talking about and this is what most receive,

It was vital for him to be made whole,

But the story I'm about to tell may be hard to believe.

My friend had a certain hope for romance not often seen,

For a long time this hope was a reality,

To find his partner early in life was his dream,

An innocent love-in all actuality.

Her smile touched not only his heart but also his soul,

Her laugh was special one that could turn gray skies blue,

Beauty made him speechless- his tongue on hold,

In all of his life he never felt something so true.

Seeing her he just knew she should be his girl,

This was that young innocent love-to him worth the wait,

Everything would mean nothing if she was not in his world,

It took a while but they soon began to date.

True love that is what he had always prayed for,

A love so deep and a girl so heavenly,

The kind of love that extended beyond his core,

He gave her his heart and told her to handle it carefully.

He gave her everything she ever needed,

A few years went by and the good times began to fade,

It's funny how love of such value can be depleted,

When he needed her love she could not come to his aid.

Together for years and she broke his heart twice,

It comes as no surprise to me why we are here today,

Years went by but the pain never sufficed,

For he gave her his heart and she went away.

So how could my friend live without his heart?

I thought I could save my friend but I was too late,

Well for a while he tried but the pain tore him apart,

There is no saving a man once his heart breaks.

I woke up in the middle of the night,

Frightened from this dream,

Trying desperately to escape the plight,

Of what I had just seen.

I began to think how easy it would be to call it quits,

For Lord knows I've been wanting to,

And how easy it would be to make a wish,

A wish for my dreams to come true.

And how easy it would be to shed a tear,

Lord knows it has been a while,

How easy it would be if love were here,

For I need to see love's smile.

How easy it would be to run away,

Lord knows it's been on my mind,

How easy it would be for me to stay,

But to stay would be a crime.

How easy it would be to end my life,

Lord knows I have been tempted,

How easy it would be to end this strife,

I leave this question open ended.

Maybe I should runaway now no one is here to see,

Do not ask me why for life is gone far too wrong,

So I pack my things and begin to flee,

For I feel like I have been gone for far too long.

I lost my purpose on this earth,

To love a girl beyond a certain span,

Without a purpose what is my worth,

Without a purpose I wonder who I am.

What is life-what is love-when you live a lie?

What is ambition shadowed only by defeat,

What is happiness when you smile but want to cry?

What is love when your heart fails to beat?

To tell you the truth I can't answer these questions,

But I've concluded now that I am living a lie,

I look in the sky praying for the Lord's blessings,

My tombstone will read "Life past him by."

And at times I wonder when I will be able to say goodbye,

Goodbye to yesterday and hello to tomorrow,

For today makes me wonder why I should try,

To live past the pain and sorrow.

Before I went to sleep one night,

I whispered this under my breath,

What followed soon was extreme plight,

I got a visit from the angel of death.

The Angel of Death

The Angel of Death came to me last night,

He told me it was time for my end,

It was hard to see past the bright white light,

I asked if he had a week to lend.

"One week," he said "that's all you receive,

So do what you will with that,"

Seven days to live I felt relieved,

"Not so fast," Death said "for I'll be back."

I packed my bags and flew home,

My parents surprised to see me,

Away I was for far too long,

Welcomed I was with glee.

But I did not come home to die,

I came home to live,

Seven days to live no need to cry,

That's more than I thought death would give.

I came back home for one main reason,

To find my meaning for life,

For my heart committed high treason,

It betrayed my soul twice.

But that's old news you've heard that story,

So focus on today,

I have a few days before I head to glory,

Listen to what I have to say.

I've heard home is where the heart is,

So I flew back to my heart,

For life without love is hard, it is,

Distance soon tore us apart.

But here I am looking at you,

As I soon approach death,

Too late it is for our love to accrue,

For I'll soon be without breath.

I came back home to find you,

To find what's been gone for a while,

To find something once old now new,

Truth be told it's in your smile.

Your smile does something to me,

Something I cannot explain,

It makes it hard for me to be,

Without you in a world filled with pain.

And your soul it is one of a kind,

I know I have been without it,

A soul I wanted to make mine,

A hole where my heart could fit.

Not only your soul but also your eyes,

Captivating they are,

At one time I did despise,

That you were no longer my star.

Aimlessly I ventured this dark world,

Hoping for re-acquaintance with light,

And now I see it's in you this girl,

I finally see that tonight.

For the first time in a while,

My world is no longer dark,

Brighten it was by your smile,

Honestly, by your heart.

So thanks for giving me life,

The week before I die,

No longer am I friends with strife,

No longer shall I cry.

Please wipe those tears from your face,

There is nothing more I can do,

Forever my heart will have a place,

Forever it will be in you.

Out of nowhere came The Angel of Life,

Hold on what are you doing here

"Your Death no longer has a price,

Your Death no longer near."

But Death told me I had a week,

"Sorry my brother sometimes acts in haste,

Truth be told I began to weep,

Because your life appeared to be a waste."

"However I see how you look at this girl,

I see what you are willing to give,

I see that you gave her your world,

I understand now why you no longer live."

"I said to death this boy you cannot kill,

He looked puzzled and asked me why,

For the past few years he's been off my will,

That means he has been dead was my reply."

"So I came to you to give you life,

Yet I see that is already done,

No longer haunted are you by death's strife,

Reunited with your heart-life has begun."

"In other words this girl saved you,

Thanks to the seeds of love planted in her heart,

A flower of love soon began to accrue,

If you want life-then never part."

So that's how my story ends,

Death I know longer knew of,

I can tell you where my life begins,

And it begins with this love.

Some dreams like this one,

Even brought me relief,

The damage had already been done,

Reality brought me grief.

For me I did not see light at the end of the tunnel,

And this made it so much harder for me,

All my lust for life is now pummeled,

Save me from my insanity.

Take me to a world free from pain,

Take me to a world where I can begin to smile,

Where hurt and sorrow no longer remain,

Lord knows such serenity has been missing for a while.

Take me to a world where my heart can grow,

Take me to a world where my heart and soul can mend,

Looking for life's next high-tired of being so low,

Never knew life could start so late only to quickly end.

Nightmares were not all I knew,

The dreams kept everything pleasant,

Although the dreams were very few,

I looked at them as a present.

From whom? Maybe a celestial being,

But I did not really care,

Reprieve I was receiving,

From pain, heartache, and despair.

The dreams greeted my grief with reprieve,

They sent hope to my despair,

Caused me to really believe,

That true love was really there.

And hope was something I needed,

It helped me survive the lonely days,

Not so fast for I pleaded,

Hoping to get past this phase.

We had a future in my dreams,

No longer did I resent the past,

So vivid it was it seemed,

That my dream would forever last.

One night I proposed to her,

The next she accepted,

Engaged we soon were,

Our love perfected.

The Proposal

I wake up with your arm across me,

Breakfast in bed I begin to make,

There you are sleep soundly,

Hurry I do for you are not wake,

This morning right here is a special one,

Years will pass but this day will not,

Soon it will be but it's just begun,

Jittering nerves my stomach in a knot,

I rush in the room with breakfast in hand,

Enter the room-you begin to wake,

Everything is going according to plan,

Here you go I said –breakfast is on the plate,

Greeted by my smile awoken by my kiss,

We converse as you eat-you make my day,

Why can't every morning be like this?

Now I have something important to say,

Or rather to ask, so please here my plea,

I prayed every day to find love anew,

For starters I know you were made for me,

An answer came personified by you,

My friends ask me is this love,

Wow they say is this true?

I respond and say you're all I think of,

A heart now mended once torn in two,

Yes they are right with you I am complete,

Now I have something to get off my chest,

Blessed I am for I no longer seek,

Another that is for I have the best,

I really do not know how to say this,

And I do not want to feel pain again,

Without you forever my heart was missed,

So this is where my proposal begins,

I get on one knee and she begins to cry,

Addicted I have become to you,

Your love has given me a brand new high,

Your love fiend I have become it's true,

Another day I shall no longer spend,

Here comes the metamorphosis of our love,

It looks as if our love has made amends,

For it was prearranged from up above.

I asked God for true love he gave me that –true,

So what shall I do with a girl so divine?

Asked God for an angel he gave me you,

The answer is to make her forever mine.

On one knee I softly take your hand,

This morning I ask you to be my wife.

Asking If I can forever be your man,

The one that loves you till the end of life.

Yes, she said without a doubt,

My Prince charming my way of life,

You are what I've dreamt about,

To God I prayed every night.

I asked for a man to love my soul,

And for years I did aimlessly roam,

To complete my life-my heart you stole,

Your heart in mine, my heart your home,

Honestly I never thought we could be,

But then I saw you were really a rare breed,

My thoughts toward love made it hard to see,

One I could love truly indeed,

You broke down these sturdy walls,

A love like this I do not deserve,

And thanks for loving me beyond my flaws,

Because for years I kept my love reserved,

Yet through it all you stayed by my side,

What an honor it is to be your bride,

Once united we will not divide,

Young we met and with love we did collide.

Fulfilling these dreams were to me,

Yet what could I do when I awake?

Save me from reality,

Save me for my own sake.

Deep down I knew none of this could be,

So it was time for me to change my view,

The life I had always wished for me,

Must now be made anew.

For I spent years,

Yearning for love's attention,

But she was never able to hear,

My heart's disposition.

It was time for a reality check,

I had to get up and shake the dust,

For far too long I had been a wreck,

For far too long in my dreams I did trust.

But that was the old me,

One who was quite innocent and naïve,

The nightmares allowed me to see,

That I would never find reprieve.

With this new found truth,

I had no choice but to change,

I know longer needed proof,

That believing in love will drive you insane.

So I say goodbye to dreams,

And yes even the fairy tales,

Life for me it seemed,

Would forever resemble hell.

REALITY CHECK

Well my friends what else can I say,

This is where I changed my mind,

There soon became no price I would pay,

To even think about making love mine.

Every now and then I would entertain,

The thought of loving again,

But I made sure to refrain,

For that stage in my life had come to an end.

Maybe I had become a pessimist,

Maybe I was wrong in end,

For in my life I had a deficit,

But my heart I had to defend.

For the past few years my heart had aged,

Now I realized something new,

That I had no choice but to turn the page,

A page with a different view.

I used to look at love in a different way,

Foolish I was to actually believe,

That fairy tales still had an important say,

In a love I wanted to conceive.

In hindsight I realize my mistake,

But moving on I won't try again,

Loving for me has come too late,

A new journey I must now begin.

As a boy I fell in love with love,

Looking for something so true,

I once thought she came from above,

Until she changed my world's view.

As a man I realize love is dead,

It hurts my soul to say,

Daily I wake up and I dread,

The love I gave away.

Lessons learned from love haunt my mind,

So beware of love's wrath,

Truth be told she once was mine,

The thought of her gone is hard to grasp.

Far too long I relied on dreams,

To help me cope with the world,

Forgetting my life wanted redeem,

Forgetting I was still without my girl.

Surprised by this reality check,

I could not figure out what to do,

My life had become such a wreck,

It was time for something new.

I renounced the love that became a lie,

In reality love does not exist,

To the fairy tales I said goodbye,

The bondage of love I did acquit.

Poetry became my way of life,

Helping me to alleviate the pain,

Allowing me to see a light,

In a world that caused my eyes to strain.

I began to see life in a different view,

Once optimism now the opposite,

The negativity in my life grew,

Until I had no good to deposit.

Cold I became to the world around me,

Maybe I took heartbreak to the extreme,

To me my heart made a plea,

Begging me to never let it dream.

To my heart I promised it this,

You will never know this pain again,

Don't worry I will not be remised,

Do this and your heart will mend.

So for once and for all,

I confronted love once more,

Tearing down the wall,

I had built to protect my core.

One more time I will be transparent,

For there I questions that have to be asked,

For it had become quite apparent,

That I needed these answers to get over my past.

I had some questions I needed to get off my chest,

Did she still love me did she still care,

It's about time that all these emotions were laid to rest,

If I needed to feel love would she be there?

Did she have feelings for me that she tried to ignore?

If I died today would she regret leaving me?

Did her love run so deeply ; did it extend beyond her core?

Turn back the time so we could be?

If we did it again would she choose to stay?

Maybe our love was too weak to light up the dark,

Or leave knowing it would be hell if we did it that way,

Did I ever make her feel something beyond her heart?

Could she feel my love deep within her soul?

Was it because of her past that we weren't together?

Does life once so filling seems like a hole?

Or were eternity and us meant to be never?

When she laid in bed at night did she begin to reminisce?

When she told me she loved me was that a lie?

Did she still remember that feeling whenever we kissed?

If she loved me so much then why the goodbye?

And now the truth is becoming more evident,

Is there a chance we will ever get back together again?

Is my dream for us now irrelevant?

Answer these questions and then my heart can mend.

Our paths collided but I've never been so far,

That day I saw my future-that's where it began,

So close to beauty yet distant how bizarre,

Where I met love only to lose her again.

But as she walked away I felt a hole,

Fair warning to all this could be a great risk,

Pursuing love was once my goal,

Now I'm here alone wishing my heart knew this.

I could shed a tear for all of my sorrow,

My past is filled with pain and regret,

But I chose to smile in hope of a better tomorrow,

Dwell on memories of her is something I neglect.

For the first time I see the start of something new,

Relationships do more harm than good,

Alone I may be but this is a breath-taking view,

To go back and change my past-I wish I could,

Temporary pain can lead to everlasting bliss,

I cannot find time for a love that is now lost,

Goodbye I say and she will be missed,

But I will find my happiness-no matter what the cost.

Was something wrong ; Was something just not right?

Sadly, there was nothing I could do to lessen the pain,

Could my problems stem from her being out of my life?

What is this life I am living now-nothing feels the same.

I feel empty now is this because dissent did accrue?

Loneliness would be an upgrade to what I am feeling,

I keep looking but whom can I turn to,

Happiness is what I want but pain is what's killing.

My eyes will never cry but my heart forever will,

I use to dream at night of what we could be,

Good riddance to her, I wish her no ill will,

Privileged she was to be loved by me.

Memories we have I wish I could erase,

I have no idea what I should do

My heart is broken can it be replaced,

Ignored it I did hoping we could make it through.

Through the good times and through the rain,

Let go and move on, I think I should,

I gave her my all-in return I got pain,

I don't love her anymore even though I said I always would.

Awaken I was with extreme hate,

Finding out that she was taken,

How much longer could I wait?

For a love that gave my dream a breaking,

I thought she no longer believed,

That love was attainable,

Sadly I was deceived,

My emotions unexplainable.

I was ready to move on,

At least that is what I thought,

Forcing myself to run,

When I should have stayed and fought.

Running caused me to be confused,

Questioning if she was still the one,

The answer I wanted but refused,

It was Love vs. Hate-and hate won.

I ran away from love so love wouldn't run away from me,

And now it has become clear to see,

That the bond I shared with her would always be,

If not, then the ghost of love would forever haunt me.

But I believed I was right and I wanted her here,

With me for I could give her better,

I promised her we would make it past her fear,

And that we would make it past the stormy weather.

Her love should belong to no other man,

For what was once one could never be two,

Sadly I was never in her plan,

Was love for us overdue?

I see how he treated her,

I promised I could do better,

I hoped I could persuade her,

With this heartfelt letter.

I could see the hurt in her eyes,

I admired her beauty from afar,

Renounce the love that had become a lie,

His love for her was quite bizarre.

Why did he treat her like this?

For she was a queen in my eyes,

She had to be careful for her life was at risk,

If her heart were to continue to cry.

Now let me explain my love for her,

Better yet let me give her a better view,

How everything could be better than what we were,

Deep down she already knew.

Now I'm a modern day Romeo

If Shakespeare was still alive,

Shot I was with cupid's arrow,

Aphrodite now weeps and cries.

For our love is more than she can conceive,

And she is the goddess of love,

Your beauty too much for her to believe,

She wonders what she has dominion of.

The goddess of love and beauty,

Now confused on what to do,

No longer has her duty,

Because of her, Aphrodite bid adieu.

And did she kiss him like she kissed me,

I could not complain and I would not deny,

When she looked in his eyes was it meant to be?

Maybe her love for me was quite a lie.

I wish it was real and I wish it were true,

So in the end what did I have to call my own,

I reminisce and had a breakthrough,

For in her I built a foundation hoping to be my home.

Silly of me I know,

But now I see that this would never be,

To love I think its best she go,

For if love made you blind quite sadly I could see.

Quite sadly I could see,

For I made a choice to say goodbye,

A choice that was best for me,

In my world love would no longer vie.

This was the hardest thing I had to do,

But it was something that had to be done,

And if you think this was a strange view,

Well the worst was yet to come.

You see I tried to trick myself,

Into thinking love no longer exist,

Truth be told it affected my health,

Could the two sides in me coexist?

Even with all of the things I could say,

One side could not help but believe,

That love would certainly be found one day,

And true love would be achieved.

One side laughed at that simple thought,

For what is not real could never be found,

One side also soon forgot,

That two souls could forever be bound.

I was split right in between,

And I knew not what to do,

Forgetting love was harder than it seemed,

The battle for my heart would soon ensue.

LOVE BIPOLAR

When it came to love I was bipolar,

One minute I love her the next I don't,

I looked at my heart and want to scold her,

One minute I let go the next I won't.

But this wasn't love this was a broken heart,

So what could I do to better my condition?

One side says love the other says part,

But one side must soon give to submission.

I do not know which way I should go,

For when it comes to love I am bipolar,

I knew love once a long time ago,

I loved her now I don't even know her.

At least I was trying not to know her,

But at times love would stop by,

And since I had become a loner,

At times love I could not deny.

I had not seen love in a while,

I tried not to look but it was too hard to resist,

As soon as I saw her my heart began to smile,

Wishing we were together for she was what I miss.

Then love would softly place her hand on my face,

Her beauty literally brought tears to my heart,

I got chills and my heart began to race,

Knowing that in moments we would be apart.

For love sure did know how to tease me,

Taken aback by her beauty I would entertain,

And even though I knew she didn't care for me,

My excitement I could not contain.

Foolishly I would try to make my case,

A case that love and I should be,

It was hard to think as my heart began to race,

It was hard to see love without me.

But I could still hear her heart calling for me

This was a feeling she could not deny,

If she was blind her heart could still see,

That we should give us another try.

I once told love that pain may bring us together,

When I first saw her I wanted her as my wife,

I said this knowing there would be stormy weather,

Yet I still wanted her forever until the end of my life.

I began to develop a neurosis,

One that only love could be the reason,

For it soon developed into a psychosis,

Where I could see my demise due to love's treason.

It became more and more apparent,

That I was tragically split in two,

My self-analysis was very arrant,

Yet still I had no clue.

For two natures were beating within my soul,

One wanted to only let go of this world,

The other could not help but hold,

Hold on to a dream that once was a girl.

One side screaming for he wants a chance to live,

Suffocating daily for he is in need of air,

The other side crying for that is something he cannot give,

One side feels hope the other feels despair.

One side wants to love and dream again,

One side lives in the past the other in the future,

The other side wants the pain only to end,

Why am I split in two-is it due to her?

My heart, my body, and my soul are living somewhere else,

Disconnected from the world in the worst way,

I look in the mirror and cannot recognize myself,

How much longer must I be left in dismay?

The weight of the world was on me,

I had to make a plea to love,

Please make sure we can never be,

This emotion I no longer want to speak of.

Forgive me love forget me too,

Unfortunately it seems she could not forget me

In the past few years I no longer know what to do,

So sit down and hear my last plea.

Forgive me love forget me too,

I gave her my all and was soon rejected,

Had to let go for she was not true,

In return I feel she should be neglected.

Forgive me love forget me too,

She lied to me-I see I was wrong,

What she owed was far overdue,

Gave her my heart but now she was gone.

Forgive me love forget me too

Love no longer exist in my world,

For now my heart is divided in two,

For she took my lover-my only girl.

And love better never come back around,

For love is a lie and I know this is true,

My friends if you think this is a bit profound,

I'm sorry but for me love never made its cue.

I wanted love to forget me,

In all honesty I think I was afraid,

Maybe it's too late to see,

Maybe my heart would be forever hazed.

For I was afraid I would love my next too much,

Afraid she would not understand,

Afraid my heart would soon be crushed,

Afraid I could not be her man.

Afraid love no longer exists,

Afraid love is no longer true,

Afraid I'm next on heartbreak's list,

Afraid my heart would stay in two.

Afraid dreams will become nightmares,

Afraid we would no longer be,

Afraid love would no longer be there,

Afraid of what I could not see.

Afraid that fairy tales were true,

Afraid she was everything I dreamt of,

Afraid she'd mend this heart in two,

Afraid of what they call love.

Years went by and I developed a fear,

A phobia of a certain emotion,

Afraid I was to let a girl near,

Afraid I was for my heart to open.

I did not realize until one day,

When I caused a girl to shed tears,

Speechless I was with nothing to say,

Causing me to wish she was still here.

I became afraid of that four letter word,

Fear did not allow me to express,

I had the noun but not the verb,

Love is what I now suppress.

Divided for I wanted love again,

But I also did despise it,

In hope-to mend my divided ends,

I'd search for a heart with plans to never find it.

Sadly, the searching caused confusion,

The girls would prepare to receive my heart,

I became a master of love's illusion,

When they were ready for love-I'd part.

Indeed it was extremely cruel,

And I'm sorry for the heart's I've broken,

But I promised to never look like a fool,

When I began to fall I'd start choking.

Cowardly, I know I am well aware,

But I am trying to make you understand,

That love in fact gave me a scare,

Bitterly I did reprimand.

Let me depict the picture,

This girl was close to perfection,

Hoped she could change my heart's fixture,

On the girl that was once my obsession.

Sadly I know you wonder,

This is not the way true love ends,

Well take a moment to ponder,

For true love did not begin.

I wanted to love her beyond time,

And maybe you thought that I could,

But the man in the mirror needed a sign,

For maybe loving her was not that good.

I saw past her imperfections,

To prolong the bonding of two,

Became a stranger to my reflection,

Causing dissent to accrue.

A heart torn in two I now see why,

For my morals I did compromise

I looked in the mirror and told a lie,

Thinking our seeds of love would soon rise.

And to the new girl I began to see,

Sadly, she came to late,

Honestly she was the better one for me,

But my past I could not negate,

This new girl, I could not look into her eyes forever,

But I could perhaps for a night,

A warning I send to prevent a sever,

With the temporary girl in my life.

We could go on dates show P.D.A.,

And even attend functions together,

Listen carefully though to what I say,

I could not look into her eyes forever.

Inevitably one day we would end,

Do not try to change my mind,

Sadly she was but just a friend,

So we better enjoy our time.

I could not look into her eyes forever,

To me she was just a replacement,

Sorry we had no future together,

Just blame my heart's displacement.

Her love for me I did not deserve,

My heart was the lowest of lows,

My love for her had been reserved,

I had been warned by Love's foes.

Easy she was on the eyes,

Do not allow love to start,

Love's foes forcing me to vie,

For the love inside her heart.

I do not deserve her love you see,

Her lips her smile her eyes,

Fail in comparison I do to thee,

To love someone like me would not be wise.

I look into her eyes and see my soul,

This she probably never heard,

In her I saw an opening hole,

For her love I did not deserve.

This temporary girl in my life,

Had a hard time trying to understand,

She had all the qualities I wanted in a wife,

But she was never part of my plan.

For I had already made a decision,

A decision to never love again,

With this girl my hate was in remission,

Because of this we came to an end.

For I chose this life this life did not choose me,

There is no four-letter word to headline tomorrow,

Love, once so vivid was now a memory,

If I claimed to have a heart it would probably be borrowed,

I choose not to love even though I wanted to try,

For I once gave away my heart with a promise of forever,

Love once existed but now it is a lie,

Love lost and long gone, give it away again? Never.

When I saw this girl,

My disposition did remain the same,

And even though she wanted to be my world,

I was afraid of the love and pain.

For sadly I realized that no girl was perfect,

A realization that came some time ago,

I would put my heart on the line if it was worth it,

How things would end I already know.

I was looking for a girl who was perfect for my heart,

Yet it seems as if this girl didn't exist,

A girl to unite with forever and never part,

A girl that I could share forever with.

Even till this day,

I look in the mirror I can see her,

Tell me what price is there to pay,

For me to forget how things were.

I could not settle for anything less than my dream girl,

Girls were knocking but I would never open the door.

But it seemed as if she only exists in a dream world,

And if that be the case I may never love once more.

FORGOTTEN LOVE

My first and only encounter with love,

Caused me to change my view,

Now a new girl I speak of,

Was trying so desperately to undo.

She wanted me to give us a try,

For she said her life I gave reason

I wanted to believe her but it was a lie,

Never fooled again by love's treason.

For I knew love once yes it's true,

Nothing last forever so love soon died,

Personified by a heart that I once knew,

Emotionally gone-physically survived.

I knew love once yes it's true,

The girl I once knew now no longer alive,

The love I had was once shared by two.

Forced me to search for what was no longer inside.

Forgotten love is what I now know,

Could I express what I feel?

Sadly the answer was a sure no,

I could not express what was not real.

I did not want to hurt anymore,

Beginning to care led to pain,

Ironically enough I closed the door,

When it came to love I wanted no claim.

So I had become a stranger,

One to myself and one to amour,

Never again facing danger,

When I found a girl to adore.

Forgotten love yes it's true,

I know longer accept it's call,

Tell me please what would you do,

To avoid love and her fall.

I wrote this not for what was but what would be,

For the past had already taken course,

But in the future I did not see,

Me ever experiencing love's force.

I had no choice but to let this girl go,

Now I realize how much I care,

Sadly for her she'll never know,

Sorry, for I knew this was not fair.

But what could I have done-love her?

No, my heart and soul knew too much despair,

So I convinced myself to dislike what we were,

Her heart too fragile-for my care.

I promise this-I did miss us,

But she came after "The One"

Now my heart no longer can trust,

Before we even start-we are done.

I never told her this face to face,

Because I was trying to make amends,

Hoping to give her a true taste,

Of what love should be-my friends.

With me she would have had no chance,

To discover a love so true,

For when it came to love –my stance,

Was such a distorted view.

Forgive me for what I have done,

As I forgive even myself,

Cowardly, when faced with love I run,

Now when I see her -I see my old self.

For I treated her,

Jut like love used to treat me,

Life could change quickly in a blur,

The tables had turned you see.

For I used to vie for love,

Back in my younger days,

Something I try not to speak of,

For that was just a phase.

But now this new girl was the old me,

And I became the new villain,

Of this emotion I was free,

But her pain made a killing.

I thought of this girl more than others,

Lost in a world unable to find me,

Wishing she was here instead of another

How long, I ask, must this be?

Truth be told I had lost my soul,

I am now a man I never wanted to be,

Moral conflicts-an emotional hole,

It took a while but I could finally see.

The truth is I could not love back,

Incapable this had become to me,

This is what I wanted and I got just that,

A life filled with pain and misery.

And to the one who came so close,

So close to bringing me to life,

I am sorry for what I did was suppose,

To never show her strife.

But reciprocate the love I'm sorry I could not,

I forgot love a long time ago,

Or maybe I was a man that love forgot,

Confused I am but there is one thing I know.

She should not fall for me, spare the heartbreak,

Or she would end up like me,

For I could not reciprocate love due to my heartache,

Cause then her heart would no longer be free.

If she loved me I would steal her heart,

Once an artist now all I do is observe

I pictured love as if it were art,

I cannot reciprocate love for her love I did not deserve.

The love I have is faded and weak,

I warned her do not love you see,

To give her my love would lead to defeat,

For I could not give her love if it no longer resided in me.

An occasional kiss-one without emotion,

But for her it would never do,

Yet for her it seemed to cause commotion,

What we once had is now through.

For I was looking for now not for later,

It's probably hard for her to understand,

Invested in love once now I hate her,

Hold on-I no longer can.

For what she wanted I could not give,

And for this I promise I'm sorry,

Her feelings for me now must sieve,

And our past must remain charry.

I wish I knew how to love again,

And honestly maybe I do,

Maybe it's best if we are no longer friends

Because for us, love never made it's cue.

WHAT IS LOVE

What is love? The question I stress,

But I will never know firsthand,

My feelings toward love have regressed,

Calling me to question who I am.

As I question love, I question myself,

Causing me to find a link between the two,

I was made to love but I need help,

To love again my heart must be made new.

Love is pure, patient, kind,

It is everything in between,

Selfless in its own design,

Let me show you what love really means.

Most people cannot love on sight,

But there are no girls like her,

I looked and said that's my wife,

A notion most girls would prefer.

I knew her before she knew me,

Had seen her before in my dreams,

A fatal attraction she soon came to be,

An angel in my eyes so it seemed.

The first stage of any love is attraction,

Beauty is something she would never lack,

Her beauty disguised as a mere distraction,

On sight she stole my heart-I needed it back.

But I let her keep it for a while,

For my heart was better in her hands,

I walked away with a slight smile,

Ready to devise my master plan.

My master plan being to delve in love,

To see if it's everything I had heard about,

This girl soon became the subject of,

A relationship I hoped to end my doubt.

How I viewed love most do not,

Love you call it, I called it something more,

Maybe through time she forgot,

How much I truly did adore.

But let me remind you, where it starts

Beware this might bring tears to your eyes,

She tried to hide since we had been apart,

But let me show you how quickly truth can become a lie.

I am out of words I know not what to say,

Love to me is now truly a lie,

Do you understand the price one must pay?

To look at love and despise.

Years of hope soon grew into doubt,

And with love doubt could not exist,

The time I wasted could never amount,

To how much she would truly be missed.

Ask me what is love I cannot tell,

I have erased the thought from my mind,

Well I've tried but memories sometimes yell,

Asking me to let them inside.

But the memory of love I kept away,

I guess that is how I cope,

Quite sadly love for me did not stay,

And now in my later years there is no hope.

Hope, I mean a second mission,

To find what I've wanted for too long,

My heart has ears but it no longer listens,

A faint cry from love I heard-but was wrong.

My heart was weakened so I let it go,

The search for the one no longer remains,

However my heart is somewhere I do not know,

I just know it's covered in a box with chains.

I do not want to find what I gave away,

For I gave it away for a reason,

I do not know till this day,

Why my heart committed high treason.

They say pain is temporary,

Well I put that adage to the test,

It seems the saying was preliminary,

Years have gone but the pain is still in my chest.

True love last forever,

For me love is pain,

Will I know happiness-never,

Love and hate are two in the same.

Now it's temporary forever,

Love is in fact a flaw,

Love can only yield a sever,

The truth did leave me in awe.

Most will never see love like I do,

What is love? To me it's a lie,

Honestly I know that's a distorted view,

Too deep in pain to even try.

Cowardly, some may say,

I do however resent that,

For in love I did continue to stay,

Only to lead my heart into a trap.

I loved her while she loved another,

Years went by and I could not understand,

How I could I love no other,

Yet she was ready to marry this man.

Make no mistake, I tried to let her go,

But she had her way of pulling me back,

Deep down I knew I would never know,

How to live if she was what I lacked.

Life has its ways of crushing my dreams,

My hopes, my wants, and my needs,

I found out one day what love really means,

When the girl that I loved-I freed.

Is it possible to love two at one time?

I asked this question over and over again,

The answer I got was truly sublime,

And that is why we came to an end.

I thought for some time my heart was divided,

Well actually that holds to be true,

What was once severed would be united,

But the love I once wanted was far overdue.

I was wrong for her heart was torn,

One side given to him, the other to me,

She had no idea what this would form,

Her divided love was not enough, you see.

If she truly loved me could you love another?

That is a question I have to ask,

For I could not find a lover,

Yet for her it was an easy task.

And I know what she had to say,

She didn't love him like she loved me,

Then why would she love him anyway,

If he was not the best –you see?

Her affection for me held her back,

I wanted her to give him her best,

I do regret my selfless act,

For there is still a pain within my chest.

And that will be there forever,

For that is how long she is gone,

A heart now completely severed,

I still wonder where we went wrong.

Maybe I should have never let her go,

I still remember that call,

She asked me why but I did not know,

Maybe I was too afraid of the fall.

I held on too long to lose her again,

And I felt that is where I was headed,

So I finally did bring us to an end,

Years have gone by and I still regret it.

A long time ago I did tell her,

I'd give her my happiness for her pain,

Earnestly I said it even though I did prefer,

To have a queen by my side to forever reign,

I wish she could have reigned with me,

But sometimes with love you have to let go,

It took me a while to finally see,

That the seeds of love sometimes never grow.

If they had, she would be here,

I'd be loving her more than she could imagine,

No need to conserve because of fear,

Limitless love, limitless passion.

What is love? To me it is sacrifice,

I let her go because of love,

For her, I would give any price,

To make sure heartache she never knew of.

Our hearts are designed for one,

And maybe I found my one too soon,

A love so promising now done,

I pray her new seeds of love bloom.

If not me then I hope he's better,

I now believe things will never be the same,

Her love for me helped to fetter,

The implosion of my heart's remains.

The thought of her kept me going,

For years and years you see,

I tried my best to keep her from knowing,

That I was still in love with she

A desperate heart will seduce the mind,

And a heart weighs more when split in two,

I knowingly gave her the bigger half of mine,

Now, love for us I no longer want it to accrue.

Nostalgia is a side effect of dying,

I heard that a long time ago,

A wish to return-I am forever trying,

Until life is what I no longer know.

Back when I had a dream,

Back when life seemed so fair,

Back when it seemed,

Love could get you anywhere.

Back when sorrow did not exist,

Back when I knew how to care,

Back when breathing wasn't a risk,

Back when my wings knew air.

Back when love had a name,

Back when smiles knew my face,

Back when I knew of no pain,

For in love's arms I was placed.

Back when I had meaning,

Back when I knew life,

Back when I was dreaming,

To wed her as my wife.

So what is love? I ask once more

She personified it for me,

I would have never known love's lore,

If she had never loved me.

What love once was is not what it is,

It is only a reminder of pain,

For what I once had is now his,

What I once wanted will never be the same.

And maybe I will get over this,

But I will never get over the shame,

For I had my heart torn led me into an abyss,,

By a girl who I gave reign.

I promised to never do that again.

I could not if I wanted to,

My past gives my future an end,

And right now I need something new.

Haunted by love or by the past,

Unable I am to continue,

I thought this would never last,

But I guess this happens when you find love is untrue.

And forever is a long time,

A duration I once wanted,

But when love is no longer mine,

Forever I am taunted.

So forever I will run,

I wish I knew how to stop,

However what's done is done,

How to love? I have forgot.

I have learned however,

To thrive in pain,

My morals now severed,

A heart no longer tamed.

And I've ran out of words,

No emotions I bare,

For my life is a blur,

I see what I want when no longer it is there.

UNREQUITED

I often feared my past would haunt me,

And so it has for a while,

It looked in my eyes and it taunted me,

Hoping to forever take my smile.

And my smile the past has taken,

Left in another time with her,

A love for me? I am mistaken,

To never know love again, I prefer.

Fair warning to you all,

Love is in fact a risk,

Many might tell you to fall,

For many cannot resist.

Never have I been one to trust,

But to her I gave my all,

In the beginning I thought love was a must,

In the beginning I was ready to fall.

Fall in love that is you see,

For love makes life worthwhile,

The better half she was to me,

The key to my heart and my smile.

How happy I was back then,

The smallest things could bring me joy,

Never did I think we'd see an end,

The pursuit of her heart was a decoy.

A trap it was I wish I had known,

I loved a girl unable to love back,

Years later and I have grown,

Into a man who loves just like that.

She taught me everything not to do,

And yet I did it anyway,

For if my heart was torn in two,

Somebody had a price to pay.

Throughout the years I have hurt others,

When really I only hurt myself,

Seeking revenge on an ex lover,

When others wanted only to help.

I never feared death but I did fear life,

A life without a love that would make me wish,

To have her as my beautiful wife,

To have a love that would forever exist.

Now those wants are gone,

And so is my lust for life,

Regrets despair and love have been thrown,

Into my sea of strife.

And the girl I owe all of this to,

I can never stop thinking of,

For she is responsible for my heart in two,

You may know her -her name is Love.

CONCLUSION

My friends in a perfect world,

In another life love may be true,

After reading this story,

Now you see why my heart's in two.

And everything I proclaimed,

You now see the reason why,

And if your view on love hasn't changed,

Well the least I did was try.

To all the hopeless romantics,

Those who think fairy tales come true,

Please get out of this game right now,

I'm trying my best to save you.

Love is a parasite,

It will suck life from you,

You'll never know it's happening,

Until the payment is due.

And what payment is this,

Well it is the hardest price to pay,

For you gave love your all,

Only to have a broken heart today.

Where are you currently?

In terms of love, what's your disposition?

Some may think it still exist,

Some may think it's their life's mission.

To love one forever,

To love one unconditionally,

To love one without the pain,

To love one without the misery.

For we all want love,

I will be the first to agree,

But if you know what's best for you,

You'd turn from love and flee.

A heartbreak from love is inevitable,

I am trying to help you understand,

Such a small pawn,

In a game with a bigger plan.

For love is a game of chess,

And as I said we are the pawns,

Love wants us to think we have a chance,

By doing this, love is a con.

When I first heard of love,

I thought it to be heavenly,

Fell in love with love,

Gave my heart away readily.

My goal with love,

Was to show the world it's true,

You see to those who think I'm lying,

I used to be just like you.

Growing up I began to see,

Love slowly dying,

Relationships all around me,

Filled with people done trying.

So I decided to show the world,

Foolishly I made this decision,

That the fairy tales come true,

To personify love was my new vision.

Yes, to all of the broken ones,

To the beaten down,

To the broken relationships,

I was ready for love's crown.

I wanted to be king,

I wanted to resurrect society,

That was filled with divorce and pain,

I wanted to rid them of sobriety.

For if there is one excuse to be drunk,

I believed we should be drunk in love,

The world needed that,

I thought this to be my calling from above.

You see my friends quite sadly,

I was once love's accomplice,

Anxiously ready to join forces with her,

Until our goal was accomplished.

The goal where we both,

Wanted to rid the world of heartache,

Where we wanted to prove,

That with love there's no heartbreak.

I was ready to do it all,

More than ready to deny,

That love was the cause for pain,

I was ready to show the world why.

Why everyone should be in love,

Why life without love is senseless,

Why the wall built around your heart,

Should forever more be defenseless.

But as with most stories,

Treachery is soon born,

I was once an ally with love,

Now the dangers of love to you I warn.

Love will embrace you,

And you will reciprocate that feeling,

For it is human nature for us,

To seek that which is most appealing.

And how can I blame you,

For love is suppose to conquer all,

Isn't that the old adage?

Isn't that what is to befall?

The myth of love,

Is that it is all we need,

For with love we have the world,

With love your life is freed.

This notion we have of love,

Where love promises us this,

That you can share your heart,

In union with pure bliss,

But love is unrequited,

Sadly I do not know why,

Had I known this in the beginning,

I'd never been love's ally.

For a quick moment,

Please imagine perfection,

The perfect life the perfect love,

What you probably felt upon inception.

You remember the bubbly feeling,

That you would get inside,

Where you could not stop smiling,

Where your feelings could no longer hide.

Maybe you were a little scared,

Maybe you told yourself to refrain,

But no matter what could be said,

You had to stake your claim.

For every ounce and fiber of your being,

Told you this was real,

This warm bubbly feeling,

Was in fact the love you feel.

Look at perfection,

Imperfect perfection at that,

For you could see some potential flaws,

But love had already started its attack.

And in that moment when you saw perfection,

Remember imperfect perfection at that,

You gave away your heart,

Hoping to never get it back.

You thought your heart,

Was better in another's hands,

But a heart not with its owner,

Is too fragile for anyone to understand.

Yet maybe you thought,

Your heart was never yours to own,

For your soul mate was born with yours,

And upon meeting, all's atoned.

So maybe with complete confidence,

You gave your heart to its rightful owner,

Finally waiting for peace,

Finally, no longer a loner.

You began to have visions,

That all in life was complete,

Where your life and your purpose,

Had ultimately come to meet.

So this is love you think,

And your lover says it is too,

Yet somewhere along the way,

Love began to trick you.

You both said you love each other,

And you all swear it wasn't a lie,

Yet a few months later,

You both are ready for goodbye.

Where did you all go wrong?

This is too much to comprehend,

Sadly when you swore to love each other,

You never saw an end.

So who is to blame?

For this centuries' old deception,

Well, I think you know the answer,

So no need to ask the question.

Allow me however,

To further remove any doubt,

For love deceived you,

Preventing your seeds of love to ever sprout.

And since the beginning of time,

This has been love's aim,

Feed the mortal's false hope,

Then tear them apart without blame.

For maybe the love we want

Truly does not exist,

But there is a thing called love,

Something we hopelessly aim for yet miss.

Say what you want about love,

But it has endured the test of time,

Although it is filled with deception,

It is immortal with the world's oldest shrine.

A shrine that sadly contains,

The broken hearts of many,

Ask me how I know this,

Well, because of love, I've seen plenty.

But the world will never tell you,

The world will never tell the truth,

For just like so many of you all,

The world needs proof.

So here I am,

Willing to give you all just that,

For the proof in my story,

Is extremely precise and exact.

And in conclusion,

I guess this story was overdue,

For you might think I am wrong,

But this story of love is true.

And everything I have proclaimed,

I hope we find common ground,

I have given you all the details,

No need for me to further expound.

For in this life and in this world,

You will begin to see,

That what everyone yearns for,

Is in fact, deadly.

Till this day,

My thoughts continue to race,

Where did I go wrong?

With love, will I forever chase?

For I know love is wrong,

But I still cannot figure out why,

I want to give this treachery,

Yet again another try.

And this paradox,

One of immense despair

For one side wants love,

Yet the other side does not care.

And the latter of the two,

This is barely alive,

For it had to lie to itself,

In order to survive.

What is the lie?

Well I have no problem repeating,

That while I don't think it's alive,

The thought of it keeps my heart beating.

And this is a lie,

That in fact the world will need,

Just promise not to get to close to love,

Admire from afar but never proceed.

For the allures of love,

Are surely unimaginable,

The depths of it,

Are truly unfathomable.

Take heed my friends,

I say this without hesitation,

Fall for the allures of love,

And your heart will experience desiccation.

If not, you will end up like me,

You will end up alone,

Where your thoughts are screaming,

For a heart you will never own.

Where your thoughts begin,

To drive you quite crazy,

Where you begin to question life,

And your dreams become hazy.

As if the world was a hammer,

And your thoughts were nails,

The constant pounding of life has now turned,

What you thought, was heaven into hell.

Surprise my friends,

This has no happy ending,

For if you have loved or ever plan to,

Your heart will soon need mending.

And I do surely hope,

That I was able to shed light,

For the sake of your dreams,

Never let them see the night.

For when nighttime comes,

You will feel this dark ominous presence

It will consume your dreams,

And destroy their effervescence.

Until you are sitting their lifeless,

For you allowed your dreams to see the night,

And once this happens dreams turn to nightmares,

Your existence followed with plight.

And this is what love will do,

It will never attack you in the light,

For all is great,

All seems right.

But once you let down your guard,

Once you begin to think dreams come true,

Love comes like a thief in the night,

For you wanted love, but it's not for you.

But this is where the story ends,

Inevitably love is pain,

The emotions you have, please rescind,

As I mentioned before love's a game.

And if you are too foolish,

To take heed to my warning,

Then I will pray for you my friend,

For your inevitable mourning.

For in the end, what is love,

But a convoluted notion,

And if you still need convincing,

Well my doors are always open.

I welcome anybody,

To disagree with me,

And if you do not now,

We can just wait and see.

For in conclusion I hope you see,

What many do not,

But if you choose to stay blind,

Your heart will soon rot.

And then you will become,

The spitting image of me,

For I chose to stay blind,

Now pain and torture is all I see.

Ask me what I think,

Well you've heard my disposition,

Love is a waste my friends,

A notion that will never receive my remission.

And even with all of this talk,

I must still continue to lie,

For love is treacherous is true,

But I can never say goodbye.

For it will make you question everything,

When it comes to love's ways,

For it is everything bad,

But it will leave you in a daze.

But one thing that,

I definitely need to get off my chest,

Love and I,

Are both truly a mess.

For love lies to you,

And causes you to see,

That dreams are wrong,

Best to stay in reality.

But deep down love knows,

That it is one of a kind,

And if it ever committed to good,

Separated souls would bind.

Love knows its allure,

But wants no part,

For in the end she could try,

Yet love is too smart.

Love came up with a plan,

To fill your wildest dreams,

To be spoken of constantly,

But very rarely seen.

By doing this,

Love creates infatuation,

Everybody wants it,

But it is never for the taken.

Then she becomes idolized,

Worshipped some would say,

But to have this life,

What price did she pay?

True love is,

Very much so adored,

By every single being,

That has room for it to be stored.

And the whole world wants her,

For with her life is complete,

Yet the quest to obtain her,

Will only lead to defeat.

She knows the truth,

But this is something she will never tell,

So she must continue to lie,

In order to put hearts in jail.

For if everyone knew love,

What would make it so unique?

If it were known by the world,

Wouldn't love lose its mystique?

And this is the problem

For love has gotten too bold,

She has the power to heal the world,

But this power she will never unfold.

And I too have lied,

I guess me and her are the same,

Yet I continue to lie to myself,

To avoid feeling shame.

For love has tricked me,

It has beaten me to near death,

Left me hopeless and alone,

Gasping desperately for breath.

For love has held me,

And told me in her I could confide,

But when it was time to talk,

Love decided to hide.

For love has promised me,

Till death do us part,

Yet when I held her to her word,

She tore my heart.

And love even had,

The audacity to say,

That with her by my side,

Pain would never come my way.

Yet the worst thing love,

Has ever done to me,

Was to show me my future,

Then say it could never be.

I even asked love,

Why would she do something so cruel?

She said to get where she is,

There is one unwritten rule.

She said never care too much,

Never lose yourself in another,

For love does exist,

And its potential unlike any other.

But a while ago

I came to a certain conclusion,

That what love could be,

Could not be experienced as human.

I look at this world she said,

And see everything in disarray,

For centuries I gave the world love,

Over time it began to decay.

Sadly I am sorry,

For I had to do what was right,

And while you might think I'm cruel,

Your passion has shown me light.

My dear old friend,

I am sorry you thought me to be a lie,

But I have a proposition for you,

One I hope that you will try.

You said you've given up on love,

For love had given up on you,

Well I think we should try once again,

To mend what was once one but now two.

A heart torn in two,

Was never what I had hoped,

You find the right girl,

And true love will evoke.

This is my promise,

I will give you your heart's desires,

But you must be willing,

To be thrown back in the fire.

Thrown back into the fire I asked,

What do you mean?

You have to risk it all again she said,

In order to achieve your dream.

And isn't that dream,

To know love in it's purest form,

Well I can give you that she said,

Then your heart reborn.

Love I said,

Thank you for your proposition,

But allow me to reiterate,

My new disposition.

I do not want to know you,

What I want in life doesn't exist,

You come to me now too late,

So your proposal I dismiss.

You did a great job,

Of showing me what could not be,

So now when I think of love,

I know this will never be.

Why are you still here I asked,

This conversation is over,

You tell me you'll give me love now,

But I'm sure there is some type of disclosure.

And even if you,

Are in fact telling the truth,

The past is still the past,

You destroyed my youth.

You destroyed a dream,

A dream I had since I was a child,

Now as I am all grown,

This dream you try to reconcile.

You said if I find the right girl,

You will give me this dream,

But even if this were true,

This girl has yet to be seen.

And even if I found her,

What do you think I would do?

Forget the past,

Because I have someone to turn to?

No, dear Love,

Even if this girl did exist,

Even if this girl were true,

Even if you did insist.

Even if I knew,

That she was the one,

I would turn from her,

Pack my things and run.

You see dear Love,

I want no part of this game,

You just promised me true love,

But I can't see past the pain.

So I rescind your offer,

Although it was extremely appealing,

To love and to be loved,

What an indescribable feeling.

But I am too lost,

Far too lost in my ways,

You think this might subside,

But this is not a phase.

I will never love again,

For this psychosis is out of control,

Something that first developed,

Because you were not there to make me whole.

Love, listen to me clearly,

I never want to see you again,

Your offer was far too late,

Now you come to me at the end?

My dream I have given up on,

And to be honest what else is new,

After my first encounter with love,

No girl on this earth is worth the woo.

But I am done with this all,

To my friends I hope you see,

That while you think you want love,

This can never be.

Maybe I spoke too much,

On my encounter with Love,

Maybe I spoke too much,

On something I should never speak of.

I am sorry for telling the truth,

For this truth is far too much to bare,

But listen to me for,

My encounter with Love was rare.

But everything I have mentioned,

Has already happened in the past,

Friends if you need help moving on,

Then you need only but ask.

Ultimately it comes down,

To one simple but complex conclusion,

How do you survive heartbreak?

Well you avoid love's illusion.

In order for me to,

To continue living in this world,

I had to get rid of the dreams and fairy tales,

Or the hopes of ever finding my girl.

And who is my girl?

Well I guess I could further explain,

For this girl I dream about,

I no longer hope to claim.

For in reality she is dead,

Not physically at all,

But mentally emotionally,

Death to my girl and her heart's call.

But for the sake of my story,

I will write once more,

A tribute to some girl out there,

Who has what I no longer hope for.

For I can say I'm sorry,

And I could bear no claim,

But I do know because of the past,

A girl's life will never be the same.

There is no love,

I have said this plenty of times,

But it is in fact a lie I tell myself,

That hurts the one who is mine.

There is a girl out there,

One that I know is for me,

But I tell myself love is dead,

In hopes that we will never be.

And I have yet to even,

Meet this beautiful girl,

Or to even share my life with her,

Or to even give her the world.

For in the end I swear this,

And I know it to be true,

That if I were to find this girl,

I would break her heart in two.

And this is why I shy away,

Shy away from love altogether,

For Love told me,

To protect my heart beyond measure.

Yes, there is a girl out there,

Who yearns to find me,

Who has hoped and dreamed,

That soul mates we'd be.

And this is where,

The true crime can be seen,

For as soon as my heart was broken,

I'd inevitably break another's dream.

For I will forever guard my heart,

And trust it in no one's hands,

The perfect girl may come along,

But she will never change my plans.

For the pain of heartache,

Is far too great a risk for me,

So I can never love again,

Even if I meet a girl as perfect as she.

And with everything that has been said,

Here lies the true tragedy,

For there is someone out there,

Who yearns to meet me.

And if they had met me,

Maybe just a little earlier in life,

We could have a chance at forever,

Where she'd reign as queen and wife.

But sadly for her,

This will never be,

The two culprits?

I guess love and me.

Now it seems that I have become,

The very thing I hate,

For I have played a part,

In a potential heartbreak.

I guess that's just how,

How the story will go,

For I will never be able to,

To allow for love to grow.

And maybe many of you can relate,

For love has lied to you as well,

Now we are stuck in life,

The definition of a living hell.

For we are the victims,

That chose to believe in a lie,

No longer are we naive,

To our hopes and dreams we say goodbye.

For the sake of this story,

There is no need for shame,

For my story and your story,

Could be one in the same.

And now we realize,

What we will soon miss,

Unrequited Love : A Heart Torn in Two,

Where Love ceased to exist.

TO BE CONTINUED…

ABOUT THE AUTHOR

Jeremy Adams started his career in writing around the age of 5. After attempting to rewrite a Bernstein Bears book and receiving low praise from his parents, he decided to pursue a career in basketball. He figured if his parents did not like his book then no one else would. Fast forward almost 20 years later after playing division 1 basketball at Texas A&M, University of Colorado, and Grand Canyon University, he has returned to his first passion-writing.

Jeremy graduated from the university of Colorado with a bachelor's degree in psychology. He soon pursued a master's degree in industrial psychology from Grand Canyon University. His master's thesis received high praise from faculty in students when he explained , in detail, the importance of each individual to look at him or herself as a business. Moreover, his focus was on self help for each individual. It may come as no surprise that his writing follows suit with his beliefs. He not only wants to help make you a better you but also help his readers understand the beauty in life through his writing.

Jeremy has spent most of his years reading countless motivational and inspirational books. It may come as no surprise that Jeremy wants his writing to help motivate and inspire his readers. Whether through poetry, novels, screenplays, or any of the above, Jeremy wants his writing to provoke thought. By provoking thought, he hopes he can make each and every one of his reader's lives a little better after reading his books.

Jeremy currently resides in Denver. Co where he continues to write. Before it is all said and done, he wants to have published at least 50 books in his life along with a few screenplays as well. For more information on Jeremy, you can subscribe to his blog adamswriter.com.

11984423R00127

Made in the USA
San Bernardino, CA
08 December 2018